D1093816

HQ
1018
.S 4
L 48
Lewis
All about families

NO RENEWAL

DATE DUE			

CHILD LIT.

Laramie County Community College
Instructional Resources Center
Cheyenne, Wyoming 82001

All About Families
the second time around

by

Helen Coale Lewis

DISCARD
L.C.C.C. LIBRARY

Illustrated by Jill Dubin

Peachtree Publishers, Ltd.

Published by
PEACHTREE PUBLISHERS, LTD.
494 Armour Circle, N.E., Atlanta, Georgia 30324

Copyright © 1980 Helen Coale Lewis, Text
Jill Dubin, Illustrations

All rights reserved. No part of this book may be produced in any form
or by any means without the prior written permission of the Publisher,
excepting brief quotes used in connection with reviews, written speci-
fically for inclusion in a magazine or newspaper.

Manufactured in the United States of America

Book and cover designed by Joan Stoliar

First Edition March 1980

Library of Congress Cataloging in Publication Data

Lewis, Helen Coale, 1944-
    All about families.

    1. Remarriage — United States. 2. Stepparents — United States.
3. Stepchildren — United States.
I. Title.
HQ1018.S4L48   306.8'7   79-26694
ISBN 0-931948-06-1

Dedicated to
Shinae and Myung
Without them, this book
would never have been written.

Contents

Introduction for Parents and Stepparents 1

Introduction for Boys and Girls 11

Words, Words, Words 15
    What Is a Stepparent?
    What Is a Stepchild?
    What About Stepbrothers and Stepsisters?
    What About Half-Brothers and Half-Sisters?
    Other Words

What's In a Name? 35
    How About Introductions?
    What About Different Last Names?

Cinderella and Other Horror Stories 45
    The Loss
    The Good Mother/Bad Mother and the Good Father/
    Bad Father
    No Replacements, Please

History 65
    Missing Information
    The Middleman
    Good Old Days
    Something Old, Something New

Instant Love, Legends and Other Myths 96
    The Myth of Instant Love
    The Loyalty Myth
    The Take-Away Myth

Special Events 109
    What Are Special-Event Days?
    Wanted: New Special-Event Days
    Little Special Events

You're on Your Own 125

Introduction
For Parents and Stepparents

This is a book for children and parents and stepparents about remarried, or second-time-around families—families in which one or both parents have been married before. In language simple enough for young children to understand it describes what the various "step" words mean and how they are different from other words used to describe relationships in families, why words like "stepmother" or "stepchild" sometimes make people uneasy, and how families can decide what names to call each other when they are not comfortable with traditional words like "mother" and "father."

It explains feelings of anger and sadness that children may have in their relationships with stepparents, it explores fantasies about the "good old days" before they had a stepparent and the fears they experience about being disloyal to their biological parents. It puts to rest the "wicked stepmother" and "poor stepchild" myths that can complicate adjustment in second-time-around families.

It suggests ways that families can be honest with one another in expressing feelings and expectations, and not hope for "instant love" between stepparents and stepchildren, recognizing that adjustments are a continual process that cannot be judged by first-time-around family yardsticks, and taking pleasure in sharing information from first-time-around family experiences which can enrich second-time-around life together.

The book is designed to help you assess honestly what you *are* in your own second-time-around family and to help you explore the many choices available to you in creating something new together—new traditions that recognize and respect the differences between first- and second-time-around families.

The messages in this book, although written simply enough for young children, are meant for all ages. It can be read by any family member alone or by all family members together.

It is not meant to be read in one sitting. How much you read each time depends on the ages of your children and the relevance of each particular section to you and your family. Because remarried families come in all shapes and sizes, not all of the material will be applicable to every family. And there will undoubtedly be things missing that might have been useful to you.

Think of the book primarily as a tool to help your family talk about important issues.

If you come to parts that make anybody in the family upset or anxious, STOP. See if you can figure out why that particular part is troublesome.

Don't demand information from anyone. Talk about things that each family member wants to share freely and honestly. We all learn from listening to other people as well as from talking ourselves.

If major issues or problems surface, ones that you feel you cannot work out yourselves, by all means look for someone who can help you—a qualified minister, family doctor, or counselor. Working out new ways of doing things is more stressful than simply following traditions inherited from the past. If you have problems, it doesn't necessarily mean that there is something wrong with you or with anyone in the family. It may simply be a matter of the numbers of situations which confront you daily for which no precedents have been set.

As I have had the privilege of working with second-time-around families professionally and experienced the personal pains and joys of being in a second-time-around family myself, I have grown to appreciate that, although people in our society are divorcing and remarrying in increasing numbers, most of what we know about family life comes from a first-time-around family tradition.

Etiquette books outline acceptable practices for marriage ceremonies and celebrations, but they do not tell us about the part children should play in a wedding when one or both adults have been married before. Books on parenthood describe how to handle sibling rivalry when a new baby is born into a family, but they don't suggest how to respond to the jealous eruptions that occur when *his* children from a first marriage and *her* children from a first marriage encounter one another as stepsiblings in *their* marriage. Books on childcare advise parents how to share the duties involved in raising children creatively and flexibly, but little is written to instruct stepparents on how to share the parenting role with their spouse, with a child's nonresident biological parent of the same sex, and, frequently, with this parent's new spouse.

There are no traditions for second-time-around families except negative ones—wicked stepmother myths, assumptions that second-time-around families are "second best," and pity for the children involved in them.

Many second-time-around families try to apply the traditions of first-time-around families to their lives, partly because that is all they have to go by and partly out of their fears about the negative traditions associated with second-time-around family life.

I remember, as I muddled through my early years as a stepparent, feeling desperate for some simple list of instructions, guaranteed to work if I but followed them, some magical "Ten Commandments of Stepparenting" that would assure me and my stepdaughters quick, painless, and successful adjustments to one another.

Looking back, I think I actually expected that one day the adjustment period would all be over and we would be just like any average, typical American family, whatever that is. I remember grinning woodenly when I was required to explain the instantaneous presence of a seven-year-old in the family and fumbling for words when I struggled with introductions; feeling defensive and guilty when she had temper tantrums and wondering what *I* had done (yes, ME, of all people, the newcomer in her life) to make her so miserable; wanting to scream at my seemingly complacent husband, THE PARENT, for the travails he and his first marriage had visited upon my life; feeling on display with extended family and friends and very guilty about the anger I felt toward my new stepdaughter.

I was apprehensive about being a stepmother rather than a mother, because nothing in my growing-up years had prepared me for the experience. When I was a child, the word "stepmother" brought visions of mean women who banished children to the confines of some lonely hearth or sent them to the ovens of witches. It never occurred to me that I would be a stepmother.

I vowed, first with one stepdaughter and then with the second, to be the best stepmother anyone could have. No kid would look at me apprehensively and wonder where I kept the poisoned apples; no grown-up would find in me subtle signs of omitted loving, because I would, of course, be instantaneously loving to both of my stepchildren.

My first stepdaughter arrived at age five as part of the marriage package, having lived for two years in her father's custody following his divorce. She had never really known her mother and had formed most of her primary emotional ties with her father and the loving extended family of grandparents, aunts, uncles, and cousins. At the time of our marriage, she was hungry for a mother and was delighted that her father had found one for her.

My second stepdaughter (two years younger than the first) arrived kicking and screaming four years later, at age seven, after living in her mother's custody and visiting us on weekends. She was not happy about the change and she let us all know it in short order!

Not having been with her for the first seven years of her life, I was somewhat handicapped by missing information. I remember the initial visit to the pediatrician with first one and then the other stepdaughter. I was aware of basic medical information—they had had their smallpox vaccinations—but the intimate knowledge that comes from soothing a child's aches and pains and rushing to hospital emergency rooms for stitches was not in my memory bank. I watched the doctor's growing frown as I answered "I don't know" to many of his questions. I imagined his well-educated brain chalking me up as a forgetful, possibly even a neglectful, mother.

"I'm their stepmother," I blurted out defensively, "so I wasn't around when all of those things happened." Did I imagine it or did his eyes cast a pitying look toward the children?

When the second grade teacher politely inquired if

the younger child's constant chattering had been a problem for her in the first grade, she didn't take too kindly to my protestations of ignorance.

"She just came to live with us," I said guiltily. Did I imagine it or did the teacher cast a protective look in my stepdaughter's direction?

With my first stepdaughter, I got by without much information. By the time of my second stepdaughter's arrival, I decided a more organized plan of action was in order.

Plan One was to use my husband as a source of information. I didn't take into account that it had been several years since he had lived with his daughter. After his fifth or sixth "I don't know" and his twentieth "That must have happened when she was two—or was it four— or was it her older sister that it happened to . . . ?" I gave up and went to Plan Two.

Plan Two consisted of my telling my husband: "Now be sure to ask her mother the next time she returns her from a visit—1) when she first went to the dentist, 2) why she still insists on a night light, 3) did she really not get to go trick-or-treating last Halloween and 4) . . . and 5) . . .."

Plan Two didn't work either. In desperation, I came up with Plan Three. I would interview my stepchildren's mother myself. I nervously called my husband's ex-wife at work and invited her to lunch. She nervously agreed to come.

Plan Three worked. Over a one-hour lunch, I asked multitudes of questions, and while I didn't get all of the answers I needed, I got more than I had ever obtained from Plans One and Two.

After that, I went to the door when she returned the children from visits and invited her in. Over coffee, I inquired about the visit, included the children in the conversation as a way of helping them change gears from one household to the other, and asked any additional questions that had come to my mind. I thought of this as a "transference of motherhood" ritual. After all, wasn't that what we were doing as the children went back and forth from one mother to another?

Armed with new information and a cordial relationship with the children's mother, I thought the difficult times were over. But they weren't.

My second stepdaughter gave me a taste of what instant motherhood is all about—temper tantrums, dramatic protestations about her change in living conditions, rosy, glowing pictures about her past life.

I did my best. I was patient and understanding, sensible and loving, but inside I was reaching the boiling point. It all began to seem rather one-sided to me. I asked myself, Why am I doing all of the trying? When is she going to try? Given the fact that I was the adult in the situation and she the child, I would have felt that a 70/30 split would have been reasonable. Why did I feel I was putting in 100 percent?

Then one day when I was being exceptionally tolerant of my stepdaughter's emotional outburst at the ice-skating rink, a close friend said, "You're just not being real."

Something inside me clicked. How could I expect my new stepdaughter to adjust to someone who was not being real? What did she sense about all of that pent-up rage and anger inside of me? What did she see in my unrealistic expectations for quick and easy adjustment? She knew, at some deep and intuitive level, that I could not "replace" a mother to whom she had been attached for seven years. She also knew that my marvelous self-control masked many feelings. Whom was I kidding?

From that point on, I became more honest with her. When she accused me of loving my other stepdaughter more than I loved her, I was able to say: "You're right. I do love her more because I have known her longer, and love is something that grows over time. One day, when you and I have had more time together, we will love each other very much."

When she shouted her anger in vicious "I hate you's," calling for her mother to come to her rescue, I was able to let her know how angry it made me to be the target for all of her rage and to tell her that her mother was not going to come rescue her; therefore, she and I would just have to work it out together—BOTH of us.

I no longer felt totally responsible for the predicaments of her life and I no longer expected our relationship to be a typical mother-daughter relationship. She and I were in this thing together and together we would have to work it out.

When I was finally able to admit to myself that our family was different—not better or worse than other families—just different, and that the difference meant there was a lot I didn't know about my stepdaughter and a lot she didn't know about me, we were out of the trees and headed for greener pastures.

It meant that I no longer had to prove myself as "good." It meant that I didn't care if she looked at me as though I had just jumped out of the pages of *Cinderella* when I sent her to her room for some transgression. It meant I could say, with utter sincerity, "We are learning to love each other and I am glad," instead of: "I love you (as much as your mother did)." It meant I could say calmly to the teacher: "That was before she came to live with us. Would you like me to call her other school and find out?"

It meant that I could relieve my husband of his need to make sure things worked out. It meant we could start laughing about how she used to hate squash and now takes three helpings, and how she used to be afraid of the dark but isn't anymore. It meant that we could begin to enjoy the ups and downs of living together as a remarried family.

I am her second mother who can never replace her first. She is my second child whom I did not come to know until she was well into childhood. When we could admit this, our real work together began—the work of coming to know and understand one another better and to learn to live together in our second-time-around family.

I look back wonderingly to my initial eagerness to put the past in the past. How could I ever have expected any of us to accomplish that? And how could I have wanted us to? The past is a part of the present and the present a part of the future in a fluid chain. To sever the chain at any point is to shorten and weaken it. And seven years is a long piece of chain from a child's point of view.

I have come to accept that there will always be things I will not understand about my stepdaughter because I wasn't part of her early life, and things that, for the same reason, she will not understand about me or her sister and father. But there is a certain richness in the frustration of all of that—an expectation that life for all of us will continue to yield surprises and challenges and hopes. And the richness could only be appreciated after we honestly acknowledged differences we have from other families and the respect and love we share for such differences. And it could only be appreciated when we all recognized that, even though both children came to the family as my husband's children and my stepchildren, they came in different ways, each with a different history and different emotional needs.

My younger one recently said to me: "Do you remember when you said love is something that grows? Ours is growing, isn't it?"

These are the touchstones of progress, solidifying

our success and bolstering us for the next crisis. For the adjustment process in second-time-around families never ends; it only changes with time.

I hope that what I have learned from my family and from the many second-time-around families who have shared their experiences with me professionally will benefit you and your family.

There is an excitement in creating something new, pioneering in this massive endeavor called remarriage and stepparenting that has flooded our American family structure with such power. Who knows what tomorrow's "typical" American family will be? Whatever it will be, your family and mine will have had a part in molding and shaping it.

Introduction

For Boys and Girls

Hello. My name is Mrs. Lewis. I am a clinical social worker. I help children and families work out problems that they are worried about in their day-to-day living. Boys and girls and their parents come to my office to talk over things that bother them and to get some help in finding new ways of doing things or thinking about things that will make them feel better. Some people call me a "family counselor" because I counsel or give advice to families.

Over the years, I have talked to many boys and girls from second-time-around families. I am part of a second-time-around family myself.

I have come to discover that millions of boys and girls in this country live in second-time-around families—families in which one parent is their parent and one parent is their stepparent.

There are many different kinds of second-time-around families.

Some children live with their mother and stepfather. Others live with their father and stepmother.

Some children have stepbrothers and stepsisters. Others do not.

Some children have lived in their second-time-around family for years; others for just a short time.

Second-time-around families are different from first-time-families—not better or worse—just different.

In first-time families, the parents who give birth to you stay married until you are grown. They are the only parents you ever have.

If one of your parents dies or if your parents get a divorce, however, the parent with whom you live may decide to get married again. This makes you part of a second-time-around family.

Most boys and girls have questions about living in a second-time-around family. They may wonder what name to call their stepparent, how to explain to their teacher about two different last names in the family, what they are supposed to do for their stepmother on Mother's Day or their stepfather on Father's Day.

Most boys and girls worry about some other things in a second-time-around family, too. They may wonder if it's okay to love both their stepfather and their father, or both their stepmother and their mother. They may feel guilty about getting mad at their stepparent or feeling jealous of him or her. They may worry about whether their parent still loves them or be afraid that their stepparent will be mean to them.

These are normal questions and normal worries. These are things that all boys and girls in second-time-around families wonder and worry about.

Sometimes, however, boys and girls feel that they are the only ones in the world who have such questions and worries. So they keep their feelings to themselves and don't talk to anyone about them. This usually makes them feel worse.

Parents and stepparents also have normal questions and worries about living in a second-time-around family. They may think that they, too, are the only parents and stepparents in the world who have such questions and worries. They can also make the mistake of not talking about their feelings.

This book is written to help boys and girls understand and talk about their normal questions and worries about second-time-around families. It is meant to help your parents and stepparents understand, also, if they decide to read the book with you.

My children and the many children who come to see me at my office have given me lots of advice about what to say to you in this book. I hope it helps you understand more about living in a second-time-around family.

Words, Words, Words

Part of the problem with the English language is that there are not enough words to use for all of the different kinds of families there are. In some languages there are more words, but in English, we have to use the same word to mean different things.

For example, the word "father" is used to describe the man who produced you biologically—the man who planted a seed inside of your mother—a seed which grew into a baby—YOU. Everyone has a father because that is the only way a baby can start to grow.

But after a baby is born, are all fathers alike? NO!

Some fathers live with their children until their children grow up and move away from home.

Some fathers leave before their children grow up.

Some fathers and mothers get a divorce and even though the father and children still see one another for visits, they don't live together any more.

Some fathers become fathers by adopting their children.

Some fathers become fathers by marrying a child's mother.

There are lots of different ways to be a father, but there is only one word, "father," for them all. There needs to be a word that stands for "father who makes you grow inside of mother," and another word for "father who makes you grow inside of mother and then goes away," and still another word for "father who doesn't live with you anymore but still sees you," or "father who isn't married to mother anymore." The plain word "father" doesn't tell you any of these things.

Here are the stories of two different fathers and their children. See what you think.

Roger's mother and father were married when they were both twenty years old. Roger's mother worked as a secretary while his father went to college to learn how to be a teacher. Roger was born just before his father graduated from college. His parents loved him very much.

When Roger was two years old, his parents began having trouble with each other. It seemed as though they were fighting all of the time. They disagreed about everything. They tried very hard to get along, but the harder they tried, the more they failed, and the more they wondered if they should stay married.

When Roger was four years old, they decided to get a divorce.

Both of them told Roger that they still loved him and would be his parents, even though they would not be married to one another anymore. They told him they knew he would miss his daddy, but he would get to see him every weekend and could talk to him on the telephone between visits.

They told him that they understood how their decision might make him angry and sad and upset.

For awhile, Roger did feel angry and sad and upset. He was mad at his father for going away and worried that he might lose his mother, too.

By the time Roger was five, he knew he could count on seeing his father *every* weekend and was no longer afraid that he would lose having a father altogether. He understood that both of his parents still loved him, even if they didn't love each other any more, and that the divorce had not been his fault.

His mother started dating other men.

She seemed happy about seeing other men, but it worried Roger. He worried that she would marry another man and that the man would try to take his father's place. Roger didn't want to lose his father because another man took over. He didn't want to lose his mother, either, to another man.

At the same time, a small part of him thought that it might be nice to have a man around the house again. A small part of him wished that his mother would get married.

When Roger was six, his mother brought home a tall man with brown, wavy hair and green eyes and a kind smile. She said to Roger: "This is Tom. He and I love each other very much and have decided to get married. I know it will take you awhile to get used to one another and become friends. Tom will be your stepfather; he will never take the place of your father, but he will help take care of you and learn to love you very much."

Over the years, Roger grew to love Tom almost as much as he loved his father (and sometimes he felt he loved him more). He called Tom "Papa" and his father he called "Dad." He proudly told his friends that he had both a father and a stepfather. He had two men who loved him and cared for him in a fatherly way—one who made him grow inside of his mother and who continued to see him and care for him after the divorce, and one who became his stepfather by marrying his mother.

Elise's parents were divorced when she was only two. Her father had lots of problems. He moved far away after the divorce and only saw Elise once. He did not help take care of her or talk to her on the telephone or come to visit her.

When Elise was four, her mother remarried. Her new stepfather was a gentle man who liked children. He spent time with Elise. He read stories to her, taught her to tie her shoes, and took her to the grocery store with him. Elise grew to love him very much. She called him "Daddy." As far as she was concerned, he was the only father she had. She knew that at one time she had had another father, the one who helped her grow inside of her mother, but she didn't remember what he looked like. Whenever people talked about him, she told them patiently that he may have been her father when she was born, but that the man she loved as a father now was the man who had taken care of her since she was four.

Can you understand why Roger loved two fathers and Elise loved one? No matter who gives birth to you, it is the person or people who take care of you, the ones who love you and whom you love, that you feel most like calling "mother" or "father." That is why Roger felt as though he had two fathers and Elise felt as though she had one.

You see, another problem with the English language is that all of the words about families are not words that say how people *feel;* they are words that say how they *should* feel. A "mother" is somebody who gives birth to you and *should* love you and take care of you. Mothers are just supposed to do that.

But what if a mother can't do that? What if she is very sick or has lots of problems? What if, because of her own problems, she can't love you and take care of you— like Elise's father couldn't take care of her? Is she still your mother? Are you supposed to love her?

Just like the word "father," there is only one word for all the different kinds of mothers there are. There should be one word for the "mother who loves you and whom you love as a mother" and another word for the "mother who gives birth to you."

There are two main things about being a mother. One is giving birth to you and the other is taking care of you and loving you. One person doesn't always do both things. And although only one mother can give birth to you, more than one mother can love you, just as Roger found out he could be loved by and could love two fathers.

There are lots of ways children can get love and care from grownups. They can get it from aunts and uncles, grandparents, friends. And they can get it from stepparents.

But once again, the English language doesn't give us enough words. There are lots of different kinds of stepmothers and stepfathers. There are women who become stepmothers to children when the children are very small, and they may be the only mothers the children ever know. There are women who don't become stepmothers until the children are practically grown up; they are more like friends to the children than mothers. There are stepparents who live with their stepchildren and stepparents who don't. There are lots of different kinds of stepparents, but there are only two words, "stepmother" and "stepfather," to use for all kinds.

I am going to tell you what each of the "step" words means in the English language. Telling you about the words doesn't tell you how you should feel or about all of the different kinds of relationships the words can stand for. It just tells you what the words mean.

What Is a Stepparent?

A stepparent is somebody who marries one of your parents. A stepmother is a woman who marries your father. A stepfather is a man who marries your mother. Their marriage is called a *remarriage* because one of them (or both of them) has been married before.

There are two main ways your Mom or Dad may marry someone other than each other: 1) if they get a *divorce* or 2) if one of them *dies*. Some parents die nowadays; many more parents get divorces.

After a death or a divorce, your Mom and Dad feel sad and angry and upset and lonely. It takes them awhile to get used to living without each other. Your Mom may start dating other men and your Dad may go out with other women. They may even try living with someone for a while.

None of the people they date or live with is your stepparent. The men your Mom dates may play ball with you or fix your toys or take you to special places. You may feel sometimes that they are acting like a father and they may feel fatherly toward you. The women your Dad goes out with may read you stories or fix your favorite dessert or give you hugs and kisses. You may feel sometimes that they are acting like a mother and they may feel motherly toward you.

If your Mom marries one of the men she has been dating, you will have a *stepfather*. If your Dad marries one of the women he has been dating, you will have a *stepmother*.

Laurie had a stepmother AND a stepfather.

Laurie's mother and father got a divorce when she was eight. Laurie's father moved to an apartment not too far away from the house where Laurie and her mother lived. Laurie visited him every weekend.

When Laurie was ten, her father married a woman named Sue. Sue became Laurie's stepmother because of her marriage to Laurie's father. Laurie still visited her father every weekend. She called Sue "my part-time stepmother" because she did not live with her.

Then when Laurie was eleven, her mother married a man named Dan. Dan became Laurie's stepfather because he married Laurie's mother. Laurie thought of him as her "full-time stepfather" because she lived with him.

Laurie lived with her mother and stepfather. Laurie visited her father and stepmother.

Do you have one stepparent or two? With whom do you live?

What Is a Stepchild?

If your mother gets married again, you will be the *stepchild* of your new stepfather. If your father gets married again, you will be the *stepchild* of your new stepmother.

You now have both parents and stepparents. You are the *child* of your parents and the *stepchild* of your stepparents.

Remember Laurie? She was the stepchild of Sue, her father's second wife, and the stepchild of Dan, her mother's second husband.

"Stepchild" is a perfectly respectable word, but most kids don't like it. That's because in the old days children became stepchildren only if one of their parents died and their other parent got married again. It always meant that they had totally lost their parent. People did not get divorces in those days. So when people knew that someone was a stepchild, they always felt sorry for them because they knew that one of their parents had died. And they told tales of horror about what "wicked" stepmothers and stepfathers did to their stepchildren. No kid wanted to be a stepchild because nobody told them about the good things that stepparents did.

In today's world, being a stepchild does mean that you have been through some upsetting times, either because of the death of one of your parents or because of their divorce. But it also means that you have another grownup, or maybe two, in your life to love you and help take care of you, and that can be good. And you are certainly not alone. There are many, many children who are stepchildren, and probably some of them go to your school or live in your neighborhood.

Think for a minute of all of the children you know who are stepchildren. Ask your parent and stepparent about all the grownups they know who are stepparents.

What About Stepbrothers and Stepsisters?

Let's suppose that Laurie's stepfather, Dan, had children from his first marriage when he married Laurie's mother. Paul, his son, was three and Karen, his daughter, was seven. When Dan married Laurie's mother and became Laurie's stepfather, Paul became Laurie's *stepbrother* and Karen, her *stepsister*.

Let's also suppose that Laurie's stepmother, Sue, had children when she married Laurie's father. She had two daughters, Ellen and Margaret. Ellen and Margaret became Laurie's *stepsisters* because their mother married Laurie's father.

Laurie had a stepbrother, Paul, and a stepsister, Karen, from her mother's second marriage and two stepsisters, Ellen and Margaret, from her father's second marriage.

If your stepparent has children when they marry your parent, the children become your stepbrothers and stepsisters. You may have stepbrothers and stepsisters in both families—your mother's new family and your father's new family. They become your stepbrothers and stepsisters when one of *their* parents marries one of *your* parents.

Becoming a "step" anything comes about only through marriage.

Do you have any stepbrothers or stepsisters?

What About Half Brothers and Half Sisters?

If your parent and stepparent have a baby together, the new baby will be your *half brother* or *half sister*. It's called "half" because half of your parents is the same and half is different.

If your mother and stepfather have a baby, you and the baby have the same mother but different fathers.

If your father and stepmother have a baby, you and the baby have the same father but different mothers.

Half has nothing to do with "better" or "worse." It is just different.

After Laurie's mother married Dan, she and Dan decided to have a baby. Laurie's mother became pregnant when Laurie had just turned twelve, and before Laurie's thirteenth birthday her mother gave birth to a baby boy. They named him Robert. Robert was Laurie's half brother because they had the same mother but different fathers. Robert was also the half brother to Paul and Karen because they had the same father but different mothers.

You have a half brother or a half sister when you have one parent who is the same and one parent who is different.

Do you have any half brothers or half sisters?

Other Words

People sometimes get other words confused with the "step" words.

Being a stepchild is not the same thing as being a _foster child._ If you are a foster child, you live with someone other than your parents—an aunt and uncle, grandparents, or maybe a family not related to you. They are your _foster parents._ You are their _foster child._ They take care of you when your own parents cannot. Foster parents may take care of you for just a few weeks (until your own parents can take care of you again) or for many years (when your own parents cannot take care of you again). Being a foster child has nothing to do with whom your parents are married to.

Do you know any foster children?

Being a stepchild is not the same thing as being an _orphan._ An orphan is someone whose parents are both dead. In the old days, before doctors knew how to cure many diseases, it was not unusual for parents to die before their children were grown, so there were many children who became orphans. Today, some children lose one parent because of death, but not many children lose both of their parents because of death. Being an orphan has nothing to do with whom your parents are married to; being an orphan means that both of your parents are dead.

Do you know any children who are orphans?

Being an *adopted child* is not the same thing as being a stepchild. If you are adopted, it means that one or both of your parents did not give birth to you but are, in *every* other way, your permanent parents. They have gone to court where a judge has made the decision to allow them to adopt you and become your parents. They are your parents because they love you and take care of you.

Do you know any adopted children?

You can be several different kinds of child with several different kinds of parents in your lifetime. You are the *child* of the parents who gave birth to you. If they get a divorce and get married again, you will be the *stepchild* of the person they marry. If your stepparent legally adopts you and becomes your permanent parent (with the permission of both of your parents) you will become their *adopted child* instead of their stepchild.

You will have been a child, a stepchild, and an adopted child.

Use this page to list all of the people in your family.

My Family

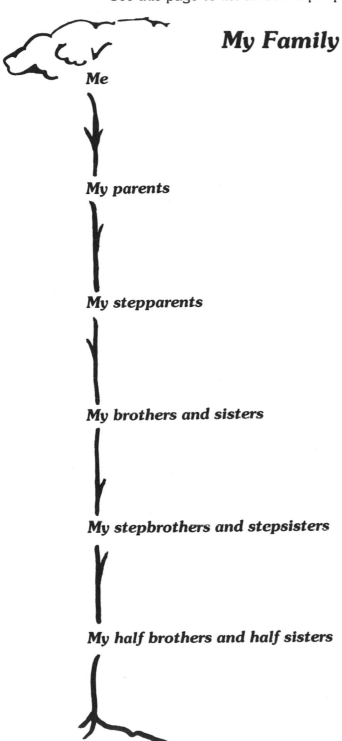

Me

My parents

My stepparents

My brothers and sisters

My stepbrothers and stepsisters

My half brothers and half sisters

Use this page to list all of the people in your family.

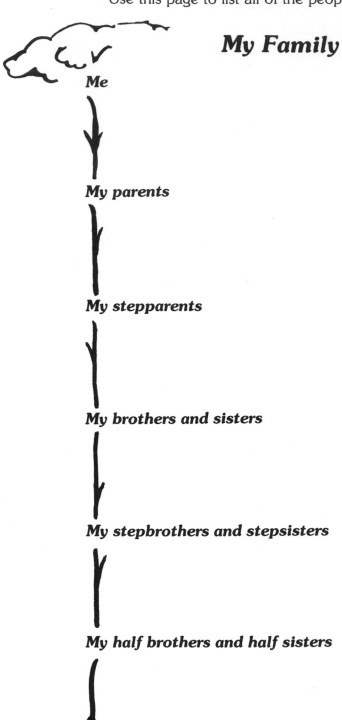

My Family

Me

My parents

My stepparents

My brothers and sisters

My stepbrothers and stepsisters

My half brothers and half sisters

Use this page to list all of the people in your family.

My Family

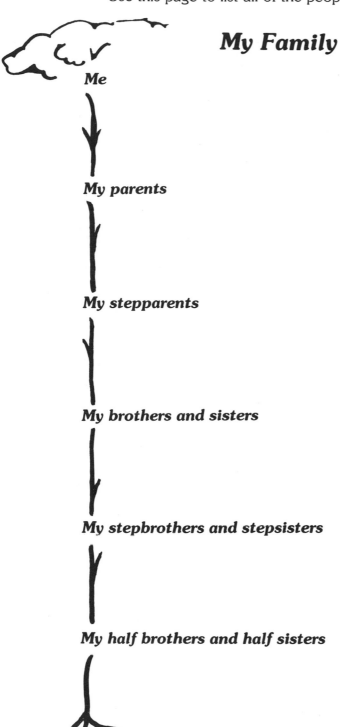

Me

My parents

My stepparents

My brothers and sisters

My stepbrothers and stepsisters

My half brothers and half sisters

Use this page to list all of the people in your family.

My Family

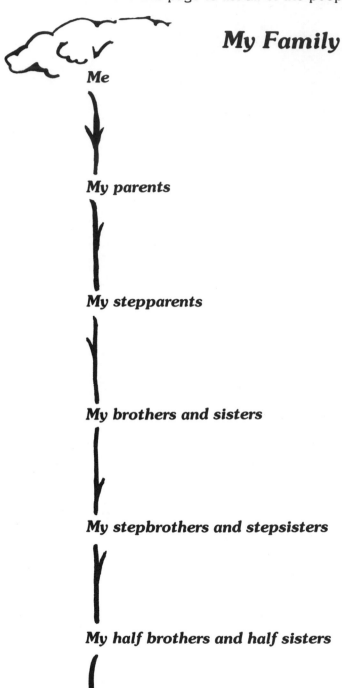

Me

My parents

My stepparents

My brothers and sisters

My stepbrothers and stepsisters

My half brothers and half sisters

What's in a Name?

Now that we have talked about what the "step" words mean, let's talk about how they are used. Are stepchildren supposed to call their stepparents "Step Mom" or "Step Dad"? What do you think?

Maybe you are comfortable calling your stepparent just plain "Mom" or "Dad." Maybe you call them by their first names—"Ann" or "John."

Some kids feel a little funny about either choice. If they use just plain "Mom" or "Dad," they feel disloyal to their real Mom or Dad. If they use their stepparent's first name, they feel uncomfortable addressing a grownup this way.

Some kids try to keep from ever calling them anything. They say "Hey you" or "she" or "him."

But this feels funny, too. It's hard to live with someone you always call "you" or "him" or "her."

Some kids think of different words. If they call their father "Dad," then they call their stepfather "Papa." If they call their mother "Mama," then they call their stepmother "Mom" or "Mummy."

The problem is that there are no official names to call a stepmother or a stepfather. That means that everyone has to make their own decisions.

Parents and stepparents can help you decide what names to use. If you haven't already done this, sit down with them and talk it over.

And you may need to try out lots of names before you decide which one feels best to you. You can use one name for a few days or a few weeks and then try another one for a few more days or weeks. Keep on trying different names until you find one that feels comfortable to you. And ask your stepparent how the names feel to them, too.

Use this page to list all of the words you have tried or might like to try calling your stepparent. Circle the ones you like best.

Names for my Stepmother   *Names for my Stepfather*

Use this page to list all of the words you have tried or might like to try calling your stepparent. Circle the ones you like best.

Names for my Stepmother

Names for my Stepfather

Use this page to list all of the words you have tried or might like to try calling your stepparent. Circle the ones you like best.

**Names for my
Stepmother**

**Names for my
Stepfather**

Use this page to list all of the words you have tried or might like to try calling your stepparent. Circle the ones you like best.

Names for my Stepmother

Names for my Stepfather

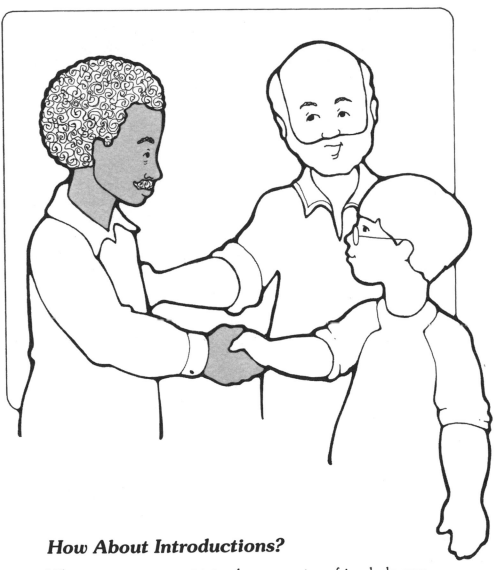

How About Introductions?

When your stepparent introduces you to a friend, do you want them to say "This is John, my stepchild" or "This is John, my wife's child" or "This is John, one of my new children"?

When you introduce your stepparent to a friend, do you want to say "This is Ralph, my Mama's new husband" or "This is my new Daddy" or "This is my stepfather"?

Again, you may have to try all of these things out and talk them over with your parent and stepparent before you decide what feels best to you. If you feel embarrassed or uncomfortable at first, that's normal. All kids feel this way while they are trying to figure these things out. And your parent and stepparent probably feel a little awkward, too, until they find the words to use.

The important thing to remember is not to keep your embarrassment and discomfort all inside of you. It doesn't go away that way—it just gets worse. So if the way you introduce your new stepparent or the way he introduces you makes you feel badly, talk it over with him and see how you can change the introductions before the next time.

What About Different Last Names?

If you live with your mother and stepfather, your mother's last name has probably changed. She and your stepfather have the same last name, but you have your father's last name.

This makes some kids feel uncomfortable. It is hard to answer the question "How come your last name is not the same as your mother's last name?"

It makes some children feel like they have to explain all the reasons their parents got a divorce and their Mom got married again—and maybe they don't want to explain it.

It makes some children want to change their last name so they don't have to answer questions about it.

It makes some children feel angry or sad or confused, like maybe it is wrong to have a different last name.

So who says all families have to be alike? Who says everyone in a family has to have the same last name? Wouldn't it be okay to have two last names on your mailbox and two last names when you sign the family Christmas cards? Whoever made the rule that *everyone* in a family should have the same last name?

Your last name is very important. It is a name that was passed down to your father from your grandfather from your great-grandfather from your great-great-grandfather. It's been around for a long time, and it carries with it lots of stories about your father's side of the family. You may just want to keep it.

You may like your stepfather's name and wish you could have it for your last name, too. You may especially wish for this if your father has gone away and doesn't see you very much and doesn't seem to love you. If this is the case (and there are some parents who aren't able to love their children), then you may not want to keep your father's last name.

The important thing is that it's okay to decide about what name you want to use, but decide about it on the basis of what you really want. Don't decide just because you get embarrassed by the questions people ask you about the different last names in your family. You don't really have to answer their questions unless you want to.

And don't decide too quickly. Changing your last name is a big decision that needs lots and lots of time and thought.

And if your parent or your stepparent is embarrassed or uncomfortable about having two last names in the family, get them to read this with you. They may need some help in understanding that two last names in a family can be fine.

Cinderella and Other Horror Stories

Most children, when they think of having a stepmother or a stepfather and of being a stepchild feel terrible. They get a scarey, sad-mad feeling deep down inside. They worry "What will happen to me?"

Perhaps they've heard of people who have had unkind stepmothers or stepfathers. Perhaps they've known other children whose stepmother or stepfather seemed nice enough but the children disliked them anyway. Perhaps they've believed all the fairy tales about "wicked" stepparents.

And there are some scarey, horrible things in fairy tales. Cinderella's stepmother made her wear rags and do all of the housework and refused to let her go to the ball. Snow White's stepmother tried to kill her with a poisoned apple because she was jealous of her beauty. A stepmother sent Hansel and Gretel into the forest to starve to death so that she would have more food for herself.

When you were small, perhaps you believed that these people were real people. Now that you are old enough to understand the difference between "real" and "pretend" you know that Cinderella and Snow White and Hansel and Gretel were not real.

But perhaps you still worry that the things that happened to them were real and could happen to children who live with a stepmother or a stepfather.

There are three things you need to understand. They are called 1) *The Loss,* 2) *The Good Mother/Bad Mother and the Good Father/Bad Father,* and 3) *No Replacements, Please.*

The Loss

One of the reasons that children can feel terrible about having a stepmother or a stepfather is that the stepmother or stepfather reminds them, just by being around, that they have lost something.

If your mother or father died or went away so that you can never see them anymore, you have lost them. You will never lose your memories of them or the fact that they were your parent. But you have lost the relationship with them. They are no longer around to love you and take care of you and help you grow into a young man or woman.

If you didn't lose your mother or father *forever,* but you don't live with them anymore, you have also lost something. They are still your mother or father and you are still their child, but you are not a family living together anymore.

Whenever you lose someone close to you, especially if it is someone very important to you, it makes you very sad and very angry and very scared. This is true whether you lose all of that person (when he dies or goes away) or just part of that person (when you see him but he doesn't live with you any more).

You feel sad because you loved them and you

wanted them to love you, in the same way that they always had, forever. You are their child and they are a big part of your life. Losing them (or part of them) is like losing a big chunk of yourself. You feel like crying a lot and you may lose your appetite or have trouble sleeping or not want to play with your friends.

This is normal. If you feel like crying, by all means, cry. And talk about how sad you are. Talk to your parent. Talk to your grandparents or your best friend. Talk about and cry about it as much as you need to.

And don't let anyone tell you not to. Grownups sometimes get worried when they see a child cry. They want him to stop because it makes them unhappy. And they say things like "Only babies cry" or "Come on and give me a big smile."

Sometimes new stepparents mistakenly think that if they were being a "good" stepparent, you wouldn't be crying.

But when you lose somebody important, it's something to cry about.

Do you still feel sad?

Another normal feeling is anger. "Why did you go away and leave me?" When people lose somebody they love, it makes them *mad*. They want to scream and shout, "How dare you leave me!" They may feel angry at the whole world, but especially at the person who left them.

Did you know that grownups feel angry, too, when somebody leaves them?

Sometimes, however, grownups worry when they see anger in children. They may say: "Don't feel that way. Your father couldn't help it that he died" or

"Getting mad won't help bring your mother back." But getting angry can help you feel better.

After all, if you lose somebody important to you, it's something to be angry about.

Do you still feel angry?

Another feeling children have is fear. They get scared when they lose one of their parents. They worry about what will happen to them if they lose their other parent, too. Or they worry about losing their stepparent.

Some children try to be as good as they know how to be so that their parent will stay. They do *everything* they are told without being asked a second time. They never pick fights with their brothers and sisters, and they are always polite and well mannered. They think mistakenly that if they are always good, they will never be left by anybody again.

Some children try to be as bad as they can be to see if that will make their parent go away. They pick fights at school; they throw screaming temper tantrums; they refuse to go to bed at night.

Being all good or all bad is no fun for anybody, child or adult.

The truth is that children don't have the kind of magical power it would take to make their parents (or their stepparents) either go away or stay. They can't make it happen by being extra good or extra bad. They can't make it happen by wishing.

Nothing they do can make it happen. If a parent dies, all the doctors in the world, with all their knowledge about how to make people well, couldn't make that parent stay alive. If one of your parents goes away, it is because your parents were having problems living together as married people.

When you lose one parent, it makes you worry about what will happen to you if you were to lose the other parent, too. And it may make you feel pretty cautious and careful about how close you want to get to a new stepparent. This is normal.

There is something you can do about that worry. You can ask your parent and your stepparent to tell you what would happen to you if you lost one of them. Perhaps you would go to live with your other parent or with your grandparents or with a favorite aunt or uncle. Most likely, you won't lose either one of them, but you need to know what will happen to you if you did. Then you won't have to spend so much time worrying about it.

You can also ask your parent and your stepparent about the sad and angry and scared feelings they have about things, too.

The Good Mother / Bad Mother and the Good Father / Bad Father

All children get angry with their parents and feel, from time to time, that their parents are bad as well as good. This is part of loving somebody. You know how you feel when your Mom or your Dad tells you "no" to something you want them to say "yes" to very much? You probably feel angry with them for awhile. You may even think to yourself: "If I lived with some other Mom and Dad, *they* wouldn't be so mean. *They'd* say 'yes' to what I want."

When you feel angry like this, you feel that your Mom or your Dad is being bad to you. These are your "Bad Mother" or "Bad Father" feelings.

Other times, you feel very happy about something your Mom or Dad has done. You love them very much and you are glad that they are your parents. These are your "Good Mother" or "Good Father" feelings.

It is normal to feel both good and bad feelings toward someone you love. All people do.

When you have both a mother and a stepmother or both a father and a stepfather, these good and bad feelings can get split in two. You may start to feel that your mother is all good and your stepmother is all bad, or that your father is all good and your stepfather is all bad. Now, instead of one mother and father to feel both loving and hateful toward, you have two—one you can love and the other you can hate.

And if you *feel* this way, you will start to *act* this way. You may give your "good" mother lots of hugs and kisses and refuse to hug your "bad" mother at all. You may wish that your "bad" father would disappear so that you can have your "good" father by himself again. Acting this way may make it hard for you to get the loving you need and want.

Grownups can split their good and bad feelings, too. If your mother talks about your father as though he were all bad and about your stepfather as though he were all good, then she is splitting her good and bad feelings. After all, your father must have had some very good qualities for her to have married him in the first place and for them to have had a child like you. And surely your stepfather has *some* faults.

The trick is to understand that no one is all "good" and no one is all "bad." Everyone is some of each. And you cannot feel only good feelings or only bad feelings toward a person without fooling yourself. You always feel some of both.

Use this space to list the things you like and the things
you don't like about each of your parents and each of
your stepparents.

Things I Like  Things I Don't Like

Mother

Stepmother

Father

Stepfather

Use this space to list the things you like and the things you don't like about each of your parents and each of your stepparents.

Things I Like   *Things I Don't Like*

Mother

Stepmother

Father

Stepfather

Use this space to list the things you like and the things you don't like about each of your parents and each of your stepparents.

Things I Like  Things I Don't Like

Mother

Stepmother

Father

Stepfather

Use this space to list the things you like and the things you don't like about each of your parents and each of your stepparents.

Things I Like  Things I Don't Like

Mother

Stepmother

Father

Stepfather

No Replacements, Please

Once you've had a mother and a father, no one can take their place. Stepparents can love you and take care of you and do lots of motherly and fatherly things for you. But they will never be exactly the same as your parents.

If you expect them to be the same, you will be disappointed.

If they expect themselves to be the same, they will be disappointed.

Suppose your mother always read you a bedtime story and this was something you liked. You expect your stepmother to do the same thing.

Suppose your stepmother doesn't like to read bedtime stories or maybe she doesn't even know you want them. But she does know lots of songs and offers to sing for you at bedtime.

You have three choices. You can: 1) tell her you don't want the songs (because you will only be satisfied with the stories that your mother always read); 2) tell her you would like to hear one of her songs; or 3) tell her you would like to read stories some nights and sing songs some nights.

If you choose number 1, you may get nothing at bedtime. If you choose number 2, you will not get exactly what your mother gave you but you may get something you will like. If you choose number 3, you may get a little bit of each.

Which choice would you make?

Suppose your father always played ball with you on Saturdays, but your stepfather is not a very good ball player. Maybe he is good at helping you with your stamp collection or making things out of wood.

If you insist that he play ball with you, just like your

father, do you think it will be fun?

If you work together on a stamp collection or make an airplane out of wood scraps, do you think you might have a better chance of having fun together?

A stepmother cannot be just like your mother. A stepfather cannot be just like your father. They can only be themselves.

You can get lots of motherly and fatherly things from them and, in some families, you may become closer to them than you are to your mother or your father. In order to know how you feel about them and how they feel about you, you have to get to know them for what they are. You get to know them better if you don't expect them to be just like your mother or father.

And if your stepparent expects himself to be able to do all of the things that your parent can do—only better —then your stepparent has to learn, too, that this won't work.

It is always better to do a good job being yourself than to try to be, or outdo, someone else.

There are no replacements, after all, in a family— only additions.

Use this page to list all of the things that you enjoy doing with your parents and with your stepparents.

Things I Like to Do

With my mother

With my stepmother

With my father

With my stepfather

With the family I live in

With the family I visit

Use this page to list all of the things that you enjoy doing with your parents and with your stepparents.

Things I Like to Do

With my mother

With my stepmother

With my father

With my stepfather

With the family I live in

With the family I visit

Use this page to list all of the things that you enjoy doing with your parents and with your stepparents.

Things I Like to Do

With my mother

With my stepmother

With my father

With my stepfather

With the family I live in

With the family I visit

Use this page to list all of the things that you enjoy doing with your parents and with your stepparents.

Things I Like to Do

With my mother

With my stepmother

With my father

With my stepfather

With the family I live in

With the family I visit

History

History is the study of the past. People like to know what happened in the world ten years ago or a hundred years ago or even a million years ago. It helps them understand why the world is the way it is and what their place is in the world. Sometimes it helps them learn from mistakes that have already been made. For example, dinosaurs were large, powerful animals with small brains that lived millions of years ago. As the world around them changed, they all died. They couldn't change fast enough to adapt. People, on the other hand, with smaller bodies and larger brains, have been able to survive all over the world, no matter how things around them changed. The study of history over the years has taught us that big brains are more important than big bodies.

Families have histories, too. Everything that happened from the time your parents were married and you were born is part of your family history. Actually, in some ways, everything that happened to your parents from the time they were born and to their parents before them is part of your family history.

Your family history includes:

Memories
Happy memories of vacations and birthdays and fun times together, sad memories of your parents' divorce or the death of one of your parents or the time the family dog got run over by a car.

Rules and Traditions
Whether you take your bath at night or in the morning, who takes you to the dentist, what kind of punishments you get when you misbehave.

Information
How much you weighed when you were born and when you had your first tetanus shot, what grades you made in first grade and where you went on your first Cub Scout trip.

Likes and Dislikes
What kinds of vegetables you enjoy and where you like to go on Saturday afternoons, the fact that Paul is your best friend and you can't stand Sharon.

All of your family history became a part of you without your even thinking about it. You just got used to it as it happened.

One of the reasons you felt badly when your parents' marriage ended was that a lot of things about your family changed. Change makes everyone uncomfortable, grownups as well as children. It means that your family history will not give you as many answers as it used to about how to live.

When your parents stopped living together, lots of things changed.

Think for a minute about all the changes you had to get used to.

Then things changed again when your parents got remarried, especially if the parent you live with is the one that got married again.

Think for a minute about some of these changes.

Think about your first family history and list some of the important things on this page. Ask your parent to help you and your stepparent to listen.

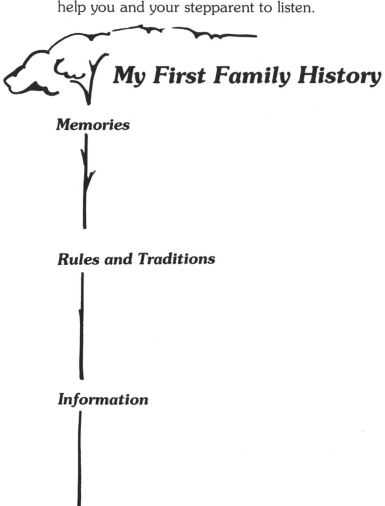

My First Family History

Memories

Rules and Traditions

Information

Likes and Dislikes

Think about your first family history and list some of the important things on this page. Ask your parent to help you and your stepparent to listen.

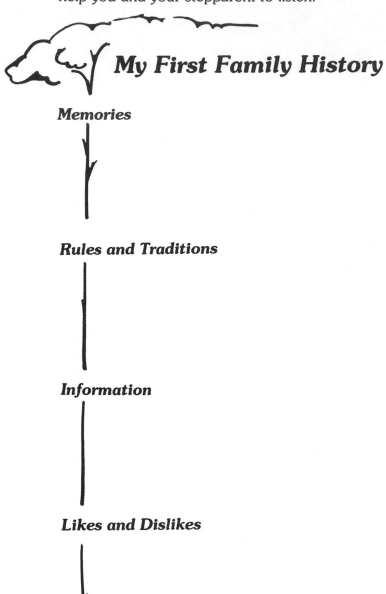

My First Family History

Memories

Rules and Traditions

Information

Likes and Dislikes

Think about your first family history and list some of the important things on this page. Ask your parent to help you and your stepparent to listen.

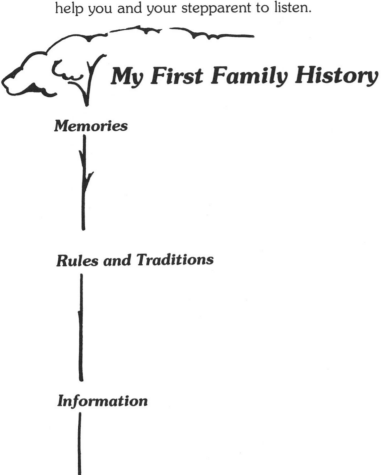

My First Family History

Memories

Rules and Traditions

Information

Likes and Dislikes

Think about your first family history and list some of
the important things on this page. Ask your parent to
help you and your stepparent to listen.

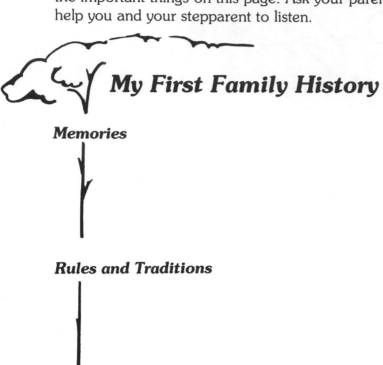

My First Family History

Memories

Rules and Traditions

Information

Likes and Dislikes

There are some important things about stepparents and family history that you need to know. They are called 1) *Missing Information,* 2) *The Middleman,* 3) *The Good Old Days,* and 4) *Something Old, Something New.*

Missing Information

Your new stepmother or stepfather knows very little about your family history. Suppose your mother married again and you have a stepfather. He only knows what your family was like from what he has been told by your mother, by friends and relatives, perhaps by your father, and by you. He wasn't around when you had your tonsils out or lost your first tooth. He doesn't know that you hate spinach and love pizza. He has a lot of *missing information.*

The older you are, the more information is missing. There is no way he can know all the things about you that your mother knows because he hasn't known you for as long. And even if there were some magical way (which there isn't) that he could find out about *every* detail of your life, it would never be the same as if he had lived it with you.

Think about all the things that are missing information for your stepparent, all the things that happened to you before he became your stepparent.

Missing information can create problems for you and for your stepparent.

Parents are supposed to know important things about their children. They are supposed to know how much they weighed when they were born and when they cut their first tooth, what grades they get in school and whether or not they are afraid of the dark. People say, if

they don't know these things, then they must not be very good parents. So right away, your stepparent has a problem—not knowing all the things about you that people say he or she should know.

This can be an uncomfortable feeling.

Missing information will mean that your stepparent will make mistakes about you, not because he doesn't like you but because he doesn't know you very well. He may put a big helping of spinach on your plate when you are used to eating only three bites. He may tell you to share your bicycle with your sister when your mother has always said that's the one thing you don't have to share. Children sometimes feel angry about their stepparents' mistakes. They may even feel the mistakes are on purpose or done to hurt them. Mainly, the mistakes are because your stepparent doesn't know what you are used to.

The best thing you can do is to help your stepparent learn about you. You can tell him you don't like spinach or have never had to share your bicycle with your sister.

This doesn't mean that your stepparent has to go along with everything you are used to, but it will help him *understand* what you are used to.

And it's a start in deciding what the rules will be in your new family.

Use this page to list all of the things you would like your stepparent to know about you.

What I'd Like My Stepparent to Know About Me

Use this page to list all of the things you would like your stepparent to know about you.

What I'd Like My Stepparent to Know About Me

Use this page to list all of the things you would like your stepparent to know about you.

What I'd Like My Stepparent to Know About Me

Use this page to list all of the things you would like your stepparent to know about you.

What I'd Like My Stepparent to Know About Me

At the same time that your stepparent is learning about you, you are learning about your stepparent.

Suppose your father always enjoyed eating a big breakfast with the family before he went to work in the morning, but your stepfather just gulps a cup of coffee, gets up from the table and hurries out the door, waving goodbye. This may make you feel bad because you think it means he doesn't want to spend any time with you in the morning. Or maybe you think it means he doesn't like your mother's cooking. You are making guesses about what he does. And the danger in making guesses is that you might make the wrong guess.

You don't know what his rushing off to work in the morning really means because you are missing a lot of information about your stepfather, just like he is missing information about you.

It will help you to ask him why he rushes out the door so quickly in the morning. Maybe he's always done it this way because he gains weight easily or can't stand to eat lots of food early in the morning or likes to spend as much time as possible sleeping. Whatever the reason, it's a part of his history and probably has nothing to do with his feelings about you.

If after he has told you why he rushes off in the morning, you would still like him to spend a little time with you before he leaves for work, then tell him. He may never eat a big breakfast like your father, but you and he may be able to work out a new way of doing things together that will become a part of your new family history.

Use this page to list all of the things you would like to know about your stepparent and about your stepbrothers and stepsisters, if you have them.

Things I Would Like to Know

About my stepmother

About my stepfather

About my stepbrothers

About my stepsisters

Use this page to list all of the things you would like to
know about your stepparent and about your stepbrothers
and stepsisters, if you have them.

Things I Would Like to Know

About my stepmother

About my stepfather

About my stepbrothers

About my stepsisters

Use this page to list all of the things you would like to know about your stepparent and about your stepbrothers and stepsisters, if you have them.

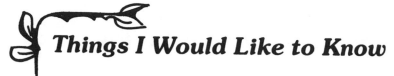

Things I Would Like to Know

About my stepmother

About my stepfather

About my stepbrothers

About my stepsisters

Use this page to list all of the things you would like to know about your stepparent and about your stepbrothers and stepsisters, if you have them.

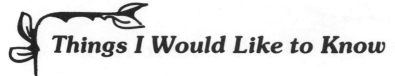

Things I Would Like to Know

About my stepmother

About my stepfather

About my stepbrothers

About my stepsisters

The Middleman

A *middleman* is someone in the middle. If I want something from you, but don't want to ask for it myself, I might ask someone else to ask you for it. I would put someone else "in the middle"—between you and me. I depend on the middleman to get from you what I want.

In our country, there are some ways that middlemen can be very helpful. If a farmer raises cows and wants to sell their milk, he has to spend a lot of time and a lot of money just taking care of his cows and getting their milk. He doesn't make the milk cartons or deliver the milk to all of the grocery stores that sell it. A middleman makes the cartons and another middleman takes the milk to the grocery stores. This helps the farmer out, but it also costs the farmer money. Each middleman gets some money for what he does and this means that the farmer does not get as much money for his milk as he would if he packaged it and took it to the store himself.

There are times when everyone needs a middleman. If the neighborhood bully starts picking on you and won't leave you alone and you have tried everything you know how to do to make him stop, you may need your mother or father to talk to the bully's mother or father. You want the bully to stop picking on you, but you can't make him stop it, so your parents become the middlemen between you and the bully.

If you want to know your mother's favorite kind of cake so that you can bake it for her as a surprise birthday present, how are you going to get this information? If you ask her yourself, she may suspect what you are going to do and then it won't be a surprise. So you ask her best friend for the flavor. The best friend becomes a middleman between you and your mother.

There are lots of situations in which people depend on middlemen. And there are lots of ways in which middlemen can be helpful.

When they are *not* helpful, however, is when they are used to supply something that should be gotten directly from the person from whom you want it. In remarried families, there is a big risk that your parent can become the middleman between you and your stepparent. And, just like the farmer with his cows, there is a price you pay when this happens.

One way you might pay a price is in getting *wrong information*. Let's go back to the breakfast example. Suppose, instead of asking your stepfather why he doesn't eat breakfast with you, you ask your mother instead. Maybe your mother knows the answer and maybe she doesn't. If you depend on her for information that only your stepfather knows for sure, you may not get the right information.

Another price you pay in using your mother as the middleman is that you will not get to know your stepfather as quickly or as well as if you asked him what you wanted to know yourself. Part of getting to know people is learning about them from what they tell you about themselves (rather than from what someone else tells you about them). So even if your mother knew the right answer, you would miss out on a chance to get to know your stepfather better.

Some mothers and fathers want their children to use them as middlemen. They say things like "Don't ask your stepfather that. I've already told you why he only drinks coffee in the morning" or "Don't ask him about going to the ball game. I'll ask him for you."

When mothers or fathers do this, it's often because they feel that the way you and your stepparent get along is up to them. They worry if you and your stepparent are angry with one another or do not seem to be getting along too well and they wonder if it's their fault.

It's not, of course. How you and your stepparent get along is between you and your stepparent. Your parent

can help out, but he or she can't make you get along. The more your parent stays out of the middle, the better off everyone in the family is.

This doesn't mean that you should never ask your parent about your stepparent. It just means that, most of the time, it's a good idea to talk to your stepparent directly, without a middleman.

Are there ways your family uses middlemen?

Good Old Days

When people talk about the "good old days," they usually are talking about a time in the past when they think things were better than they are today. People talk about the "good old days" of horses and buggies before there were cars and traffic jams and air pollution. They talk about the "good old days" of home-grown food when everybody had their own vegetable garden and there was no such thing as frozen food.

If you asked most people if they would trade in their cars for horses and buggies or the convenience of frozen foods for a vegetable garden, they would say "no." They recognize that, while it was enjoyable to ride slowly in a horse and buggy without worrying about traffic jams and pollution, it also meant that you couldn't go very many places, especially if they were far away. And, while home-grown foods tasted delicious, they also took a lot of time and work to prepare and they weren't available year round like today's frozen foods are.

Even if they recognized all this and still yearned for the "good old days," they couldn't have them. The "good old days" are in the past and will never be here in the same way again.

There were good things and bad things about the old days, just like there are good things and bad things about today.

Suppose someone didn't understand this (and there are some people who don't). Suppose they said "Everything about horses and buggies was better than the cars we have today." If they really believed this, what do you think they would do? Maybe they would refuse to ride in cars altogether, or if they did ride, they would complain about the traffic and the pollution all the time they were in the car. They would never enjoy going anywhere because they would always be wishing they were in a horse and buggy instead. Pretty soon, other

people wouldn't want to ride with them. Perhaps they would ride in a car only when they absolutely had to (to a doctor's appointment or to the grocery store) and would never use a car for fun things like trips to the beach or to see their friends. They would miss a lot, wouldn't they? They would be playing the "good old days" game, only they wouldn't be having very much fun.

People can play the "good old days" game in families, too. Think back for a minute about your family history, when your parents were married to each other. Think of all the good things and all the bad things. Think of all the things you liked and all the things you didn't like.

If you can only remember the good things, then you may be playing the "good old days" game. And just like the person who found all good with the horse and buggy and all bad with today's cars, you may be missing a lot.

There are good and bad things about all families. If your parents' marriage ended in divorce, one or both of your parents felt that the marriage was more bad than good. If the marriage ended because one of your parents died, it may have been mostly good with only a little bad. Or it may have been the other way around. No matter how the marriage ended between your parents, there was some good and some bad.

Does anyone in your family play the "good old days" game?

Something Old, Something New

As you live together and get to know one another, you and your parent and your stepparent and, if you have them, your stepbrothers and stepsisters, are making a family history of your own. Everyone in the family has a family history that they brought with them to the family,

so part of the family history is "old"—from before you were a family together. And part of the family history is "new"—all the things you are working out each day since you have been together as a family.

Your family history will include the same kinds of things that you brought with you from your first family— memories, rules and traditions, information, and likes and dislikes. Only all of these things will be a mixture of old and new. How much you weighed when you were born and when you cut your first tooth are things that will never change. They are part of the first family history. Where you go on family vacations and how much allowance you get will be new—part of the history you are making together in your remarried family. The longer you have lived together the more new family history there will be.

Think for a minute about some of the new family history you and your family are making together. Ask your parent and your stepparent about it, too.

Instant Love, Legends and Other Myths

A legend is a story that got started a long time ago and, although it's only partly true or maybe not even true at all, it is believed to be true by many people.

The story of *Johnny Appleseed* is a kind of story known as a "legend." Johnny Appleseed, according to the story, planted thousands of apple trees all over the eastern and midwestern parts of the United States. You and I know that no one person could have planted all of those trees, especially during the days when the only form of transportation was your own two legs or a horse and there was no fancy machinery to help a person plant things. But the legend says that Johnny Appleseed walked all over the country planting trees.

This legend is true in part. There was a man named Johnny Chapman who loved apple trees so much that he walked around planting them everywhere he could. People who lived in the nearby towns saw him coming and going every few weeks with his big bag of seeds and wondered what he was doing. Pretty soon the word got around that he was planting apple seeds and, not knowing his name, the townspeople started calling him "Johnny Appleseed." Whenever they saw him coming, they would say to each other "Here comes Johnny Appleseed again, planting his apple trees." And the townspeople told their children about him and their children told their children and pretty soon everyone had heard about Johnny Appleseed. That's how we got that legend.

Myths get started with part-truths, too. Have you ever heard the superstitious saying "If you step on a crack, you'll break your mother's back"?

You know and I know that that's not true. Stepping on cracks is not the way backs get broken. But have you ever stepped on a crack and worried—just a little bit—that when you saw your mother, her back might be broken?

Probably one day a long time ago, some little girl was playing jump rope or hopscotch or some other game when she was supposed to be helping her mother peel the potatoes or hang up the laundry. Her mother kept calling to her and, one time, she said, "Susie, I declare, you're going to break my back with all of this work if you don't come and help me." And Susie, heading into the house to help her mother, wondered if she had the power to break her mother's back. While she was peeling the potatoes, she thought up the rhyme, "If you step on a crack, you'll break your mother's back." It made a nice jump rope rhyme, so she taught it to the other kids at school and, before you knew it, everyone was jumping rope to it. And, as they walked home from school, they tried not to step on any cracks just in case it was true.

There are lots of myths about families. In families where there are stepparents and stepchildren, there is 1) *The Myth of Instant Love,* 2) *The Loyalty Myth,* and 3) *The Take-Away Myth.*

The Myth of Instant Love

People say that parents are supposed to love their children and children are supposed to love their parents. Most parents and children do love each other. They love each other because they *learn* to love each other. Love grows as you get to know someone. You get to know their good points and their bad points. Love is not something that happens right away as soon as you meet someone. It is a myth to think that love comes in an instant.

When you were first born, your mother and father were probably amazed at you—how little and cute all your fingers and toes were, how pretty your eyes were, how loudly you could scream when you were hungry or wet. They didn't know you very well at first, because you had just been born, but they felt a lot of things about you. They were happy to welcome you into this world, scared about whether they would be able to take care of you the way they wanted to, worried about whether or not you were healthy, cross sometimes at the way you woke them up during the middle of the night, curious about what you would be like as you grew up. They felt lots of things.

As they lived with you and took care of you and watched you grow, they began to love you. And each year you've been around, their love for you has grown. And each year you've been around, you've been growing in your love for your parents, too.

This doesn't mean that you love everything about them or that they love everything about you. There are things you like and things you don't like and things they like and things they don't like. This is part of loving.

When you live in a family with a stepparent, love operates the same way. Your stepparent does not love you right away and you don't love your stepparent right away.

And if you tell each other at the beginning that you love each other, somewhere, deep down inside of you, it doesn't feel right because you know it's not true. You may want it to be true and your stepparent may want it to be true, but saying it won't make it so. There is no such thing as instant love.

Love is something that can grow between you and your stepparent as you get to know one another, as you do things together, and as you tell one another your feelings. So if you don't love your stepparent right away and if your stepparent doesn't love you right away, remember that that is normal. It takes time for love to grow.

If you have stepbrothers and stepsisters, your stepparent will have different feelings for them than for you. Suppose you have a stepfather who has children—your stepbrothers and stepsisters. Your stepfather has known his children for a long time, long enough for love to grow. He has known them for a lot longer than he has known you, so it's only normal that he will love them more than he will love you and that they will love him more than you love him.

Your mother, on the other hand, has known you a lot longer than she has known his children. She will love you more than she loves them and you will love her more than they love her. This is normal. It has nothing to do with how lovable you are as a person. It's just that it takes love a while to grow.

Some families get into trouble with each other by trying to make everything "equal." They try to be sure that everybody loves everybody else all the same. If a mother tells her children "I love you," then she feels she has to tell her stepchildren the same thing. If a stepfather loves his children, he feels he must love his stepchildren in the same amount.

Love can't be divided up into equal parts that way, and when people try to do it, it doesn't work. It's not real. After several years of living together, a stepfather may love his stepchildren as much as his children and a stepchild may love his stepfather as much as his father. This is because there has been time for love to grow.

When that happens, it feels good.

The Loyalty Myth

In the old days, people could get their heads cut off or be put in dungeons for not being loyal to their King and Queen. If someone did anything that the King or Queen thought was not loyal—WHHT! Off with their head!

The idea was that *every* person had *one* King and Queen to love and serve. And they couldn't love and serve more than one. If they did, something was wrong with them and they were punished.

Some of our ideas about mothers and fathers are like the old ideas about Kings and Queens. You are supposed to love lots of people (aunts and uncles, grandparents, good friends), but you are only supposed to love one person as your father and one person as your mother. If you love anyone else as much, then you are thought to be disloyal to your mother and father.

This isn't true, of course. That's why it's called the *Loyalty Myth.*

There is nothing horrible that happens to you if you love a mother and a stepmother or a father and a stepfather. You are not being disloyal. It can be kind of nice to have extra parents to love and be loved by. A lot of children like that.

But what if you don't love your father and you do love your stepfather? Or if you don't love your mother and you do love your stepmother? Maybe you feel you should love your parent at least as much as your stepparent (and probably more). And you worry and feel guilty that you love your stepparent more.

Remember, you learn to love people not just because they are your mother or your father, but because you have learned to love them for the *kind of person they are.* If your father left after the divorce and hardly *ever sees* you, and your stepfather is around all the time and helps take good care of you, of course you love your stepfather more than your father. If your mother died when you were very small and you have known your stepmother for a long time (and she takes good care of you), of course you love your stepmother more than your mother.

Unfortunately, not all parents understand this. Your mother may get angry if she thinks you are learning to love your stepmother. Your stepfather may say bad things about your father as a way of trying to make you love him less. If this happens to you—if any of your parents or stepparents try to make you love someone less than you do—then they need help in understanding how love grows.

The Take-Away Myth

Another word for "subtract" is "take-away." Ten "subtract" five is five. Ten "take away" five is five. If you subtract or take away, you have less than you started with.

Some children feel that when their parents get remarried, it's like subtraction or take away. They fear the stepparent will take away their parent's love and they will have less of that love than they started with. Sometimes, they worry that they will have worse than less love—they are afraid they will have no love at all.

This is not true.

When two people get married, they have to spend a lot of time and energy getting used to living together. If *he* is used to celebrating Christmas on Christmas Eve and *she* is used to celebrating it on Christmas Day, they have to decide when *they* will celebrate Christmas. If he does not like to cook and she wants some help with the cooking, they have to decide what to do about mealtimes. There are lots of things that have to be decided. And deciding all of these things will take a lot of their time. This means that you will have less time with

your parent than you are used to, but it doesn't mean that your parent's love has been taken away from you.

Also since your parents' marriage ended, you may not have been used to seeing your mother kiss and hug anyone but you. Now she kisses and hugs your stepfather and that makes you jealous. You worry that her kissing and hugging him means that she loves you less than she used to. Perhaps you feel very angry at him because it seems as though he has taken away your mother's love from you. He hasn't, of course, but it feels that way.

Love is a funny thing. It grows between people in lots of different ways. And there are lots of different kinds of love. There is love between good friends. There is love between parents and children. There is love between husbands and wives. Each kind of love is different—not better or worse—just different.

The hard thing to understand is that love is not something that gets smaller as you spread it around. It gets bigger. The better your mother and stepfather love each other, the better they will be·able to love you. The better you love your parents and stepparents and other important people in your life, the better you will be able to love your husband or wife when you grow up and get married.

If you worry about losing your mother's love to a stepfather or your father's love to a stepmother, one thing you can do about that worry is to talk to them about it. You can ask them if they love you less than they did before they got married. And if they say to you (as grownups sometimes do), "Of course I don't love you any less. Whatever made you think that?," don't stop there. Ask them "What about the time when I wanted you to read me a story and you went to bed early to watch television with your new husband?" or "How come you hug and kiss him all the time and you don't do it to me as much any more?" Keep on asking all of the

questions you need to ask until you feel less worried about it. It's a normal worry. All children feel it, and if your parent and stepparent are reading this book with you, they will understand that you need to ask these questions.

Instant Love, Legends and Other Myths   107

Special Events

There are some days out of the year that are special. They are special because of what they stand for.

Most special days stand for things that are enjoyable and fun to think about.

Some special days stand for things that are sad and not much fun to think about.

What Are Special-Event Days?

In the United States, July 4th is a special day that most people enjoy because it is the day we celebrate our country's independence, the day we officially became a country over two hundred years ago. Some people call July 4th our country's birthday. There are usually fireworks and picnics and lots of parades—things that help us celebrate and have fun.

Another special-event day in the United States is Memorial Day. This is a day that makes many people sad because it is the day set aside by our government to remember and honor all the American men and women who have died in wars. There are no fireworks on Memorial Day because it is not meant to be a happy day.

Churches and synagogues have special-event days, too—Christmas and Easter, Hanukkah and Passover.

And birthdays and anniversaries are special-event days for families.

Will you think for a minute of all the special-event days you have celebrated? Make a list of them.

Special Events List

Will you think for a minute of all the special-event days you have celebrated? Make a list of them.

Special Events List

Will you think for a minute of all the special-event days
you have celebrated? Make a list of them.

Special Events List

Will you think for a minute of all the special-event days you have celebrated? Make a list of them.

Special Events List

Now go back over your list and think of the ways you like to celebrate each of the special-event days. What kind of food do you like to eat? Do you like to go somewhere to celebrate or do you like to stay home? Are there special decorations that you like to put up? What kind of clothes do you wear? What time of day do you celebrate? Do you exchange gifts? What people are included in the celebration?

Every family has its own ways of celebrating, even though they may be celebrating the same special-event day.

In Sean's family, for example, birthdays are always celebrated with a big birthday party. Each year about two weeks before his birthday, Sean and his mother go shopping for birthday party invitations, crepe paper decorations to hang from the ceiling, balloons and noisemakers, prizes for games, candy, and birthday napkins and paper plates. Sean's mother asks Sean what kind of cake and ice cream he wants to have and what kind of games he wants to play. She helps him address the invitations to his friends. On the day of his party, Sean has about fifteen children with him at his house to help him celebrate. They bring presents, eat cake and ice cream, and play games for several hours. Sean enjoys celebrating his birthday with his friends, and because he has always celebrated this way, it would seen strange to do it any other way.

Louisa's family has always believed that birthdays are a special family day. Louisa's mother says that birthdays are to celebrate the day a person becomes a member of a family, and they should be celebrated just with the family. Every year on her birthday, Louisa gets to choose what she will have for breakfast, lunch, and dinner. It is *her* day and the whole family has to eat what she decides. She also gets to pick two special activities to do with the family—picnics, bike rides, ice skating, a trip to the movies—whatever she wants within the choices her parents give her. In the evening, she receives presents from her parents and from her older brother. Sometimes her grandparents come by to visit and give her their birthday wishes. Louisa enjoys her birthdays. She has celebrated them with her family for so many years that any other way would seem strange to her.

What do you think would happen if Sean's father and Louisa's mother got married? Would Sean still celebrate his birthday the same way? Would Louisa?

Sean's father might not know how Louisa got to pick the family meals and activities on her birthday, and he might suggest that she invite lots of children over for a party. Louisa's mother might not know that Sean always had a big party on his birthday and she might suggest that Sean celebrate his birthday just with the family. Sean and Louisa might both feel sad and angry that their birthdays were not celebrated the way they used to be. Sean might think that his new stepmother didn't really like him or care about what he wanted. Louisa might think that her new stepfather didn't really like her or care what she wanted.

If you were Sean or Louisa, what would you do?

There are so many differences in the ways that families celebrate special days that no two families are ever exactly alike. When two families join forces to become one, through remarriage, they have to learn all of the different ways they have each celebrated special days. Then they have to decide which ways they, as a new family, will celebrate. The only way this can happen is if they talk about each special day, how they celebrated it in the past, and how they want to celebrate it in the future. Sean and Louisa could help their new family decide about birthdays if they sat down with their parent and stepparent and told them what they liked and how they felt.

Decisions must also be made about special-event days that involve the parent you don't live with. Who will take you shopping to buy a present for their birthday? Will they be invited to the family party to celebrate your graduation? What part of the spring holidays will you get to spend with them? Who will take you to their wedding if and when they get married again?

Because these are special events, most children who visit with their parent want to celebrate some things with them. To do this takes some planning.

If you have thought about some of these questions but don't know the answers to them, now is the time to talk them over with the parent and the stepparent with whom you live.

Wanted: New Special-Event Days

There are some special-event days that, no matter how you and your new family decide to celebrate them, something may not feel right about it.

Mother's Day and Father's Day can be like that. If you have a stepfather, what do you do on Father's Day?

Some children have known their stepmother or their stepfather so long and feel so close to them that they are happy celebrating Mother's Day or Father's Day with them. They like giving them presents and cards that say "To the best mother (or father) a kid could have."

Some children have known their stepmother or their stepfather for only a short time and do not feel as close to them as they do to their own mother or father. What are they supposed to do on Mother's Day and Father's Day? Are they just supposed to ignore it, even though

they might like their stepmother or stepfather and want to show them in some way that they care? Are they supposed to make up their own card that says "To a very nice stepmother" or "To a fine stepfather"?

We need a new special-event day—a STEPPARENT DAY—when all the children with stepparents could recognize them with cards and gifts meant just for stepparents.

Or perhaps what we need is a STEPFAMILY DAY, when all of the parents, children, stepparents and stepchildren who are in remarried families could celebrate the joining together of their two families into one. There could be presents exchanged and special food and cards that say "It hasn't always been easy, but I'm glad we're all in the same family." There would be advertisements in all the stores "Hurry and get your presents for STEPFAMILY DAY while the supplies last" and teachers would help children make presents at school. The day could be set aside each year in middle January, just after the old year has blended into the new.

Just think of it—stepfamilies with their own holiday celebration!

If you were going to plan a STEPFAMILY DAY for your family, what would you do? Ask your parent and stepparent and anybody else that lives in your family for their ideas, too.

Little Special Events

All families have little special events as well as big ones. They usually don't set aside whole days or plan big celebrations for the little special events, but they do take note of them.

Some parents, for example, glue a tape measure to the wall and mark on it how many inches you have grown every year. When they measure you, they say "Look how much you've grown since last year! Remember when you only came up to my waist? Now you are much taller!"

Some parents say "I remember when you couldn't tie your own shoes or get dressed by yourself. Now you do a fine job with both." Or "Remember when you used to come inside crying every time Roger hit you and now you know how to handle bullies like him?"

Little special events happen between husbands and wives, too. They sometimes say to each other "Remember when we used to worry about paying our bills every month? It's nice to be able to afford more things now." Or "Remember when we used to fight every time your sister came to visit? I'm glad we're getting along better now."

These are all little special events—important things that happen as husbands and wives and parents and children live together and watch each other grow and change.

In remarried families, little special events are important, too. They are all the things that grow and change, with time, as you and your parent and your stepparent and other members of your family live together.

List the little "special events" that have occurred since you first became a second-time-around family.

Little Special Events List

List the little "special events" that have occurred since
you first became a second-time-around family.

Little Special Events List

List the little "special events" that have occurred since you first became a second-time-around family.

Little Special Events List

List the little "special events" that have occurred since
you first became a second-time-around family.

 **Little Special Events List**

You're on Your Own

This is where you get to make your own chapter in the book. You may want to take your pick of any of the following suggestions:

Paste in photographs of everyone in your family or draw pictures of them.

Write a story about your family.

Make a list of the questions you still have about any members of your family.

Make up a poem about stepfamilies.

Ask everybody in the family to write something about the family and how it feels to be a member of it.

OR . . .

Write anything else that you would like added to this book.

YOU'RE ON YOUR OWN!